# HISTORY OF THE TASMANIAN VORTEX

by Earthkeeper Barbara Susan Christiansen

# ACKNOWLEDGEMENTS

Gratitude to Michael for teaching me how to listen.
And much thanks to Carol Matthews for front cover design.

The photographs in the book are Sue Christiansen originals and have been saved over many years.

This edition first published in 2018
by Vortex Publishing
215 Dalmayne Road
Gray TAS 7215
Australia

Copyright Barbara Susan Christiansen
All rights reserved. No part of this publication may be reproduced, stored in a retrieval system, or transmitted in any form or by any means, electronic, mechanical, photocopying, recording, or otherwise, without the prior written permission of the Publisher and copyright holders.

"Sue's journey has been one of Faith and Trust, listening to her calling and Creating the Vortex Healing Centre. The journey continues... "Grandmother Beth Davies

"A well written narrative concerning her spiritual calling to establish the Vortex at St Mary's, Tasmania. She listened, and now runs a thriving healing center."
Author Carolyn Wyrsch

"An enlightening joyous and fulfilling journey of discovery and how the Author's life is guided by signs and symbolic happenings! Fascinating read. I wanted more!"
Karen Polden

# Table of Contents

Prologue..................................................................................2
The Journey Begins................................................................3
Changes.................................................................................. 9
Tasmania................................................................................12
A Rent, a Mortgage and No Income........................................14
Egypt...................................................................................... 19
*Junitta and Tassie Sue at the base of Pyramids*......................21
The First Diamond.................................................................24
2008: A Very Big Year............................................................28
Back to Egypt......................................................................... 40
The Great Pyramids...............................................................49
The Two Become One............................................................52
What Next? Mission Impossible!............................................55
Adjustments...........................................................................58
Birth of the Vortex Healing Centre........................................63
11/11/2011............................................................................. 69
Stage One Complete!..............................................................72
Afterword............................................................................... 75

# Prologue

I stood on what is now known as the Tasmanian Sea Mounts and looked towards the east coast of Tasmania. There was a glow on the mountainside and I knew I would return, sometime in the very distant future, to restore that glow.

I looked at the Golden Sun Disk I held, and touched the engravings, absorbing the light knowledge that emanated from the disk.

I placed it carefully knowing my work was done. Lemuria was sinking. I gazed again at the glow on the mountainside and whispered, "I will return."

# The Journey Begins

My journey began with a crack on the head, when a horse fell over backwards on me. My head split open in my helmet and I had a jagged line across my vision for half an hour or so. Sixteen stitches later I was sent home to rest.

Somehow the fall had awakened my psychic abilities (of which I knew nothing at the time). I was hearing voices as I went to sleep and faces appeared through a pink background. If that wasn't bad enough I smelled incense everywhere, so strong sometimes that I thought it was right under my nose. I don't have a sense of smell... compliments of a broken nose. Night after night I would be prowling around the house looking for fire!

Admittedly I was in a very sensitive state after recently breaking up with my "happily ever after"

but...
I feared a padded cell was waiting for me!

My life, until now, had been a fun-filled adventure with me living my passion. Horses had been my life and I had done great things including becoming one of the first Lady Jockeys. A group of women got together and fought the VRC (Victorian Racing Club), and after seven years we were granted restricted licences to ride in races. We were restricted to country races against one another. However we proved our worth. I only rode in three races due to a weight problem, but I won all of them. We paved the way for the next generation!

With the parting of my "happily ever after", life became a lot more difficult, the rose-coloured glasses came off and reality set in. Financial difficulties, plus being unable to ride for a few weeks, took its toll on my bank balance, and a whiplash in a car prang added to my woes.

I couldn't ride for a while so desperate measures had me cleaning out a lot of horse stables to survive, and the smoke and voices hadn't gone away.

I was talking to my sister-in-law and mentioned that I was seeing and smelling things. Very brave of me as I had told no one up until then. She just laughed and said, "Don't worry, you are just psychic!"

Huh? "What is that?" I said.

Long story short, she invited me over to meet her mother who knew all about this stuff. Hmmm, well she blew my head off! She introduced me to a whole new world, one which I realised was happening before my fall, but which dealt with stuff I had chosen to ignore. From here my life took a radical turn. She had recommended a Scottish psychic who was a member of the Spiritualist Church. All my warning bells were going off. *Agghhhh,* a cult/religion, no way...

My sister had come to live with me for a bit to help out with my finances, and she convinced me to go and see the psychic. Hmmmm, "Not without you," I said.

We went and my life took another turn. The visit absolutely floored me! I had taken my neck brace off and left it in the car, and after introducing herself, she commented on my sore neck and back and said she would give me a healing after our reading. My eyes grew bigger, and that was just the beginning. She told us many things she couldn't possibly have known. Robyn and I grew quieter and quieter.

Then she told me about a sick horse I had and said because I was a healer, I could fix her.

"No, I train horses, that is what I do," I protested.

She chuckled and went on to tell me about the sick horse. She told me the iron I was feeding her wasn't working and I needed to inject it. OK, she had my interest now as my horse was not getting better.

"She has a blockage in her bowel and if you put your hands on her she will get better," she told me.

"But I pat her every day," was my rather pathetic reply.

"It will be different now," she said.

She then got me to sit in front of her and she put her hands on my neck. I waited patiently for her to do something but she never moved. Her hands were nice and warm though.

We went back home and had some wine. We wondered how she knew all that stuff about us.

The next morning I got out of bed and thought, gee that hurt, and then I thought, no it didn't! I got back in bed and tried it again. It still didn't hurt... Robyn got woken up to me touching my toes.

"I need coffee," she said and then realised what I was trying to show her.

We went out to "heal" the horse. I pushed up my sleeves and said, "Abracadabra you are healed."

Robyn growled at me to do it properly, but I didn't know how!

I was patting the horse on her tummy as I talked to Robyn and the next minute she leapt in the air (the horse not Robyn) and burped, which horses cannot do. She took off bucking around the paddock, and then she came back and started to lick me as if saying thank you. We wondered if it was too early for some more wine!

Two days later, I was hanging out the washing and the "sick" horse came galloping up to the fence, turned around and started to do a pooh!

"Good one Blondie," I said, and she grunted. "Bit constipated are we dear?" I asked.

Another grunt and a look that said *LOOK*, so I did and there was a square of greaseproof paper coming out. Some school kid had thrown their uneaten lunch in her paddock and she had eaten it all. That was her blockage! Yes folks, I had to be hit in the face literally!

OK I AM NOW LISTENING!

I went inside and rang my Scottish sledgehammer, and she answered by saying, "I have been waiting for your call."

# Changes

In three short months my life had radically changed. I started a Naturopathy course, to learn all I could about healing. I read hundreds of esoteric books to learn about healing, and I joined a group with my Scottish sledgehammer. Wow, I hadn't even realised that I had stopped smelling things. It seemed it was guardian angel who had been trying to comfort me by showing me I was not alone, and I still smell incense when I need to take notice of something.

Three years later, I had moved away from racing and horses, and I opened a clinic in my old home town of Phillip Island. I had found that very few people wanted to do the hard work to change their lives, and just wanted pills to fix them. I had taken a massage course to complement my work and specialised in this. My healing gift was working and I learnt so much from this time. I was also shown how to fix most things in the body with special techniques.

I met my mentor around about that time, and he was responsible for my life taking yet another turn. I was so pleased with my life and the work I had done to get where I was, that I was unprepared for my mentor to say, "The first thing we will do is get rid of all your beliefs. They are getting in the way WHAT! I worked very hard for my beliefs!

So, he did just that, worked away until I did realise the limitations I had placed on my learning more about me. Hmmm. He would come in and sleep through a massage and leave me with a most ridiculous statement, for me to figure out how he came to that conclusion. He taught me how to think.

My practice grew and once again my sister joined me and discovered her own healing gift. She went on and did clinical hypnosis and was an absolute wonder at a technique called Myofacial release, which released emotions as well as muscles!

During this time I took a short break in Tasmania, and after being there two days I knew that someday I would live here; in fact it became a burning goal.

On Phillip Island, we ended up with a very good business with many coming from as far away as Melbourne.

Then my mother got sick and died from an inoperable cancer. I was not prepared for the impact this would have on my life. Mum had been a great believer in the things I had done; and a great encouragement. Her wisdom was earthy and real, and I still needed her. At the same time my dog got sick and had to be put down, and I broke my toe chopping wood through tears and yells. It was time for a break.

# Tasmania

I hopped on to the small plane that went from Phillip Island to Tasmania, and thought I was going there to prepare for a retreat I had organised. I had gone a couple of days early to unwind and figure out what clients needed from their retreat.

I had had a swim and spa and a lovely Chinese meal and had settled for the night in bed in front of the TV. I was getting a drink when a big white arrow came out of my heart.

Oh dear. More padded cell material! It got bigger and I was aware of a Kaditcha man (Aboriginal healer/wise man) in my peripheral vision.

A map of Tasmania appeared before me and the arrow pointed to a spot on the map! Woohoo! My next adventure was unfolding. I had been looking for land but on the north coast, and the arrow was pointing to the east coast.

How I ended up with this beautiful land is a

long story. It will be in my other book along with many of the details I have left out here.

The land was on a mountain side overlooking the sea. It was beautiful, even if it was a cow paddock and the bracken was as tall as me. I knew it was the right place so I lied to the bank and bought it.

There was a slump in the building trade on Phillip Island so that took a huge chunk of my usual income from massaging out of reach.

However, a dispute over the title took twelve months to fix, so by the time I started paying the mortgage my income was good again. My father hadn't coped very well with the loss of Mum and dementia settled in. It would be another four years before I could move to Tassie.

Many trips to my land in Tasmania kept me sane, opened me up to the beauty of nature once more, and more fine tuning from my mentor gave me little time to think of the future.

But eventually it arrived.

# A Rent, a Mortgage and No Income

I needed to sell my house on Phillip Island in order to build in Tassie, but it didn't happen. It was too cold to camp on the land, so I rented in the town of St Helens, which I chose due to it having the bigger population than my local town of St Marys.

I thought work would flow but it didn't. Tasmanians hadn't caught up with the wonderful benefits of massage. "Do I really have to take my clothes off?"

I took an overdraft and it filled quickly. Finally my house rented out and that eased the pressure. Dad was nearing the end of his life and I had been able to move here because he didn't know if we were there every day. He still knew us but the TV had more interest.

Throughout Dad's dementia he gave us our inheritance. I had paid off the mortgage on my house to buy the Tassie land, so it was back to a mortgage, and a rent and little income.

I survived, and my house eventually sold but at a much lower price than I hoped for. This meant another loan to build my dream home.

I had bought an old builder's caravan to put on the land and had parked it in front of the huge laurel tree, out of sight of the road. My first night saw me hop into bed and wonder why the roof was purple. I was very refreshed though I had little sleep and I guessed I had parked on a ley line. I got out my trusty coat-hanger which I use as a dowser, and sure enough there was a ley line going right under my bed!

The land was waking up! A ley line is like the energy meridians in our bodies, and this was a positive one. My work was starting! I connected with the line and my heart surged; the energy was very strong. I also connected with the Aboriginal caretakers of the land (in spirit) and they welcomed me to be the physical caretaker. (I had to prove first that I was a suitable earthkeeper.)

I invited my dear old friend of twenty years to come and visit me.

When she first got there she wandered off while I lit the gas in the caravan. She called me over and wanted me to talk to the huge black snake she was talking to. I kept my distance but as I looked over to her I saw that the dead tree had fallen, (this tree was the area where I had picked up on the

Aboriginal pain). Many aboriginals had been hunted and shot. Tasmania has a shameful past with the first peoples of this beautiful Island.

I called Junitta over and just before we got to the tree there was a small orchid and its shape was of female genitalia. Junitta was jumping around in excitement. A black snake, the fallen tree and the female orchid combined in a great omen; the snake meaning new growth, the fallen tree the healing of the Aboriginal pain here, and the female orchid was the future; the female energy of the planet was destined to be returned! (The energy has been a patriarchal or male energy on Earth for centuries.)

The land was growing! The ley line was now about a foot wide, it was only a few inches wide when I found it.

As the frequencies grew with the growth of the ley line and land, I too had to grow. This involved the shedding of emotions that had been stored, so lots of tears and anger went through me on a regular basis. My meditation group I had started also grew, and each solstice and equinox we were doing a ceremony. This would help download all the newest energies into the ley line.

The first nine years in Tasmania saw me very short of money. My dream home got built to lockup stage, and as soon as the water was connected, I moved in! There was no power, no hot water and no heat, but luckily it was still warm.

I went to put my dog in the kennels for the day as she had taken advantage of our lack of fences and started following me. I was telling the guy I was going to Launceston to buy a woodstove, if I could afford one (it was wishful thinking on my part), and he said that he could build me a heater, with a hot plate and a hot water heater in it. I could have kissed him!

My dream home was a round house and a mezzanine floor for the bedroom. It was a simple but wonderful, cheap-to-build, home.

I had also started to work at the Lymphoedema clinic in St Marys, so income was slowly picking up. I would go home and paint a wall and sing to the sixties channel, one of two that my radio could pick up.

The ABC, it seems, is available everywhere and I spent many wonderful evenings with Australian talk-back. It was a wonderful time in my life.

After three years I had saved enough to line the ceiling, but I remembered that there was no wiring for power. The ceiling had to wait and two years later my house had a solar system installed. What an invention! After five years without power, I could turn a light on, so no more candles.

I actually mourned the loss of that stage of my journey.

The energy on the planet was due to change and a friend who had been staying with me and I stood on the ley line the day the energy was to change. We both got a huge bolt of energy that bent us double. It was amazing. We dowsed the ley line and sure enough the coat-hanger swung to the left ~ female~. It had always swung to the right before.

# Egypt

Egypt was always on my bucket list and suddenly I thought that I was fifty, so I had better go to Egypt! As I do, that night I found a suitable trip and thought I had better ring Junitta as she knows so much about Egypt and most other things, than I do.

When she answered I said, "I am going to Egypt. Do you want to come?"

"No," she said and hung up.

I thought I would give her half an hour but ten minutes later, she rang back and said OK!

Three weeks later we set off.

Our first stop was Aswan, a beautiful place but most of us got a bug the next day as we flew up to see the Temple of Isis. I did miss this but Junitta had a great day. I never ever get a cough normally, but I did this time and it was bad.

We were in Cairo and heading into the Great Pyramid the next day. I chose not to disrupt the group with my coughing and stayed behind. The next day was a free day so I could go into the pyramid then. Junitta reported getting a huge download in the King's Chamber. It was to go into volcanoes she said.

The next day we both set off to go into the pyramid, but Junitta felt she had to walk the base while I went inside. I was surprised to find the King's chamber all to myself, and the vibes were amazing. I knew I had something to do so I tuned in and asked.

Just coat the pyramid with the female energy, I was told. Uh how? As usual, no answer!

A thought field would not be strong enough I thought so I asked for help and an Egyptian appeared in my mind's eye with a candle that had two wicks. OK, that may work, so I lit the candle and put it on top of the pyramid and watched the beeswax melt down the sides. Yes that should stick, I concluded, and the vision disappeared.

*Junitta and Tassie Sue at the base of Pyramids*

Junitta had walked the base and set the energies. She was also waving and laughing but I couldn't figure out why. I was so high when I came out that I was walking into a machine gun and its handler.

We also had an amazing connection with Akhenaten in the Egyptian museum. Little did I know that this connection would call me back in 2009.

Back home Junitta came over for the Winter Solstice and said she had done her duty and downloaded her pyramid energy. However she was aware that she had more to download so I pointed out that St Patricks Head was a volcanic cone, and that is the Pyramid of St Marys, and also visible from the Vortex. Paddy's Head is also visible from the land.

About this time I found another ley line that crossed the first and it had formed a small vortex where the two crossed.

We gathered a couple of friends and this time I set the base and Junitta did the inside work. The energy was downloaded into the Vortex in what Junitta described as an egg. I had placed a small clear quartz on each corner and when we looked at them they had a flash of blue in them.

This meant that the Sirians were working with this download, as they did in Egypt during the reign of Akhenaten.

I watched the egg with my inner eye and could see that it was slowly rising. Over a few weeks it rose above the Vortex and I could clearly see Quan Yin inside. The divine mother was birthed through the Vortex! Quan Yin is often seen and felt here and many feel the touch of her hand upon their cheeks. Quan Yin guides the Vortex area and brings those who need the Vortex special energies. One of these was a Maori Elder called Kiri Dewes. She was to have a huge impact on my life at a much later date. I love the way seeds get sown!

The ley line had grown to about twenty feet wide, and all those who visited could feel it. The energy rises to the solar plexus and beyond, but it is a solar plexus portal. The energies therefore are very healing as they work with the seat of the self. The benefits of visiting ley lines are many but the main one is that you draw the higher vibrating energy up through your own energy meridians, which activates any DNA codes that are set to open at that frequency. If you visit a lower vibrating area then the energy is downloaded, through you, to the area. This is why I get sent to many of the sacred sites that have been polluted through misuse, or misguided people directing energy. I carry the high vibration of the divine mother from the Tasmanian Vortex.

# The First Diamond

The energies of the Vortex were now quite high as my group continued our ceremonies. The great Shift was being talked about in all the spiritual circles, as it had been since the Harmonic Convergence in 1984. We were feeling a lot of changes within ourselves, and in the Vortex area, we were buzzing. This usually means something big is coming!

One meditation night I saw a huge citrine-coloured diamond hovering above the group. It stayed the whole evening. I knew I was supposed to do something with it, but what?

A few days later I emailed my friend Celia Fenn. Celia channelled Archangel Michael and her writings have kept me on the true path many a time. She emailed back within ten minutes and her excitement was evident. They had been waiting for the arrival of the first diamond to go into the newly forming diamond grid. WOW what an honour! Tassie had got the first (first known) diamond.

My group downloaded the huge diamond on the 7/7/2007. Ceila and her friends oversaw the activation of the diamond on the 11/7/2007. As we activated it the diamond began to slowly spin. Our crystals, which we had placed on the Vortex, started to glow.

The light was clearly coming from beneath it. The sun had not risen yet.

What an honour for Tasmania to receive the first Diamond in the new grid! It was citrine-coloured because the Vortex was a Solar Plexus portal.

The ley line got a lot wider, and after doing some research I realized that we were on the tail of the Great Rainbow Serpent line that went through most of the power sites on the planet. A lot of these sites I had visited or sent energised crystals to, so there was a spider web of energy going to and from the Tasmanian Vortex. The isolation of the Vortex had kept it in pristine condition. As far as I knew there had been only one other resident family and they had hand-carved a stone house. Many of the stones still remain, and the foundations are now under the huge laurel tree, which they would have planted in their back yard. Their name was Kringle and they had ten children, so a lot of good vibes there!

I had also discovered a male vortex about fifty yards away from the female one. I felt that one day the two would join and balance the energies.

*Crystal glowing with light on the Vortex*

## 2008: A Very Big Year

I had come across a website called Earthkeeper.com and really resonated with the writings. James Tyberonne was the Earthkeeper, and I plucked up the courage to ask him about the direction the Tasmanian Vortex would take.

He responded in ten minutes and replied, "Congratulations, you are the first of our spiritual family to answer the call. We had agreed to meet in Peru in 2008 on the March equinox, and to do some work there. Are you coming?"

Not the answer I expected! However, I can never resist a dangling carrot!

"How much?" I asked as my finances were still very shaky.

He told me the cost and my heart sank. No way I could afford that, so I replied, "OK, I will be there!"

Who could resist that invitation?

James also sent me a requested reading from Lord Metaton, whom he channels, and wow, was that amazing!

It seemed I was to meet an aspect of myself in Peru; one of our family. An aspect is part of the greater you in a different body. We have between eight to sixteen aspects incarnate at the same time. This was going to be a very interesting trip!

I have a genetic disorder call Primary Lymphoedema, which means I can't get rid of all my lymph fluid. It gets worse on planes and high altitude. This is why I never really made it as a jockey as I had to lose up to 7 and a half kilos to ride for every race.

OK, I had a few months to get fit and so twice a day I rode the exercise bike for half an hour. This moves the fluid more than any other method. After three weeks I had put on two kgs. This is normal for a lymphoedema person as the fat burned off now fills the space with fluid. After six weeks I had lost most of that and was feeling quite fit. When I left for Peru I had lost six kgs!

I had expected the money to come. You know; via the *if you are supposed to go the money will come* thesis. Well it didn't but I maxed the bankcard and got on the plane!

I left a day early to try to remove the fluid build-up that happens on the long flight. Twenty-one hours later, I fell into bed in Peru. I had packed fat clothes mainly, as the research I had done on lymphoedema shows an increase in fluid in high atmospheric conditions. I found I was the exception and lost so much fluid in the first few days that I went everywhere holding my pants up!

Eleven women and Tyb went on the trip, as two other males had dropped out. It was amazing meeting my family. They seemed like old friends but I found no obvious aspect.

As I was about to learn, all my trips have a twist. I had been looking at Tyb and sensing there was something that needed to be done. I had no idea what, but it kept bugging me so I eventually spoke to this huge bear of a man.

"OK," he said, "let me know when," and he walked off. As I was very shy, my heart was pounding as it took great courage to tell someone who is leagues ahead of me that we have some work to do.

It seemed Tyb had been a priest at Machu Picchu during the time it was evacuated. He was responsible for taking some of the scrolls of sacred knowledge away. He was killed in a rock fall in the escape tunnels and the knowledge remained there. We had to retrieve it so the work we needed to do would get done.

Most of our group opted to climb Wayan Picchu, but I had decided to have some quiet time at the hitching post, a landmark at Machu Picchu.

I was on my own at six in the morning and placed my crystals to charge on the stone there. I took a photo, and then sat down to meditate.

A bee kept buzzing but I ignored it and blissed out for a bit, but the buzzing grew louder so I opened my eyes and it was doing a figure of eight right in front of my eyes. Hmmm.

I looked up and my hawk totem was circling above. OK, it was time!

I found Tyb and told him what I had figured out and that it was time to retrieve the knowledge.

He said, "That sounds right, but I have a huge claustrophobia to overcome."

We sat down and meditated and I led him through to the tunnel, but he couldn't get there. I saw some of our group wandering towards us, and I smiled. Help was coming! I quickly explained and together we got Tyb through the tunnel and he retrieved the scrolls. The knowledge was released and I suddenly saw a rope ladder swinging in front of me.

Lord Metaron's voice boomed out, saying, "Tell them what you see Sue!"

"Ah a rope ladder.... could it be DNA?"

Oh duh! Yes!

Machu Picchu was set to become the new spiritual centre of the planet as Mount Kalesh (the current spiritual centre) was suffering with the

Chinese invasion. We released the knowledge to enable Machu Picchu's DNA to be upgraded!

Woohoo, what a buzz! When I looked at my photos that night, there was a shadow of an alien in the hitching post picture; a Sirian! I was not alone. My guide was with me!

*Hitching Post at Machu Picchu. I am not alone!*

It was a fabulous trip with plenty more highlights,

especially the Ayhausca and San Pedro experience. This too is in my other book, as it is not relevant for the Vortex story.

I took the upgraded energies back and downloaded them into the Vortex. I had also connected with the Sun Disk at Lake Titicaca and bought those energies back! I did manage to connect with my aspect. Her name is also Barbara and we left a day early to catch planes back home; New Jersey and Tasmania!

As she left in the taxi to the airport, she turned and waved. Damn! I thought. That is her!

We kept in contact and became great friends.

Finding an aspect of yourself is a huge adventure and great for seeing what you could have become with different circumstances. It is like looking in the mirror at a stranger that has the same mannerisms, and faults and good points. What a roller-coaster of a ride it was getting to know Barbara. I learned so much more about myself!

We explored this relationship from different sides of the planet and as our friendship grew we decided that a trip to Mount Shasta on the 8/8/2008 would be in order. Tyb's reading had suggested I visit there.

When you work in the spiritual realms, a chance is never wasted, so I was asked to download a diamond into the newly forming grid under the Earth.

I had discussed this with Barbara and she was keen so we set off up the mountain. Everyone had told us that Panther Meadows was the big energy site, and we duly found a spot that was energetically bubbling. We set out our protective diamond and the etheric diamond settled into the earth. As we did this I saw the City of Light in Tasmania lift from the earth and then a figure of 8 with a vesica piscies in the middle appeared. It also had spikes all around it. I laughingly said to Barbara that this symbol would be a crop circle the next day.

As in most cases we knew we had to come back in a few days and activate the diamond.

We checked out the area, had a lovely walk and headed back to Stewart Springs where we were staying. We had passed through a flock of butterflies on the way up and saw a few on the way back. Our car number plate was 88, and we were also in room 8. We were quite happy with ourselves we enjoyed a bath in the mineral waters.

The next morning we had breakfast at our favourite diner in Weed. All was good until the Shekinah or divine female decided to take residence in Barbara.

I have experienced the divine feminine so was

quite comfortable with her energies, but Barbara couldn't stop laughing or crying. Movement was hysterically funny, and her long legs seemed to have a mind of their own. One minute she was walking beside me; the next she was fifty metres ahead and still laughing hysterically.

This continued on and off during the next two days.

"I can drive," she said, but next minute came the hysterical laughter as she couldn't find the gear stick.

I drove!

It was time to head back up the mountain, but we managed to drive past all the gas stations even though we knew we needed gas/petrol. We didn't have enough to get up the top so we thought we had better turn around and go back for petrol. Looking for a place to turn we came upon another flock of butterflies.

Hmmmm, I thought, so we pulled over and followed them. They led us to a vortex and wow it was huge. As my role is as an earthkeeper, a huge download happened into the vortex and I was nearly knocked over by the strength of it. I then saw in my mind's eye, some Lemurians (light bodied people who live beneath Mount Shasta and various other places including Tasmania), and they were dragging a sled with the diamond we had downloaded the other day. It seems we should have followed the butterflies the first day, not the human opinions! It was placed in the Vortex and was soon starting to rotate. Barbara was waving her arms in the air thinking she was doing another Shekinah lack of control, but I believe she was weaving the ethers over the Vortex.

We headed back to Sonoma where Barbara had some wine business to do. Not much was said as we let all we had done settle.

The next morning I looked up the Crop Circle Website and sure enough there was the symbol we had seen. The look on Barbara's face was amusing to say the least.

*Crop Circle on the 8th of the 8th of 2008*

I had dreamt that we were going to meet another aspect of ourselves, but he hadn't appeared. I thought he was some kind of Shaman. We went to a barbecue at a winemaker friend of Barbara's place and as we walked in I nudged Barbara and said, "That's him!"

"Who?" she said.

"Our aspect," I replied and as I said that he turned around and gave me a hug and said, "Great to see you again."

Again, the look on Barbara's face was priceless!

We all ended up in the spa at our hotel later that evening. He had been bought up by his gypsy mum so he knew all about the "other worlds". He had chosen a different path and was happy. He looked a lot like my sister. We talked for ages, and then parted.

In that same dream, I was also told that Barbara was going to go through a huge transformation, and Shekinah was as big as you get!

Barbara had been given a huge initiation into my world. How would she handle all of it?

More visits to Tasmania!

The Vortex continued to grow and with the new connections it was becoming very powerful.

# Back to Egypt

How do you follow a year like that? I was happily massaging at work, pondering life, when a thought banged into my consciousness.
This year is a true 11/11/11; a pure triple master number. 11+11+200 +9. Where should I be on the highest vibrating day of the year? Well the highest vibrating place on the planet, I believe, is the King's Chamber in the great Pyramid in Egypt.
　My client stirred and I realized he was a travel agent.
　Woohoo! Back to Egypt!
　A group of eleven signed up and I enlisted Barbara's help to organise it. We had eleven from Australia, and an American and an English woman were to join us when we arrived in Cairo.
　We got picked up at the airport to be taken to the airport hotel before flying to Luxor the next day. We drove straight past it and ended up in the Nile Hilton in the middle of Cairo. We were assured the two internationals would be brought

here when they arrived; just a change of plans, he said.

Exhausted, we went to our rooms to get some sleep after nineteen hours in the air.

Just as I smiled and snuggled down, Akhenaten popped in and said, "I want you at the museum when it opens tomorrow morning."

Knowing what the queues were like to get in the museum, I rang everyone's rooms and said, "Early start."

It seemed my connection with Ahkenaton last trip was going to be continued. Hmm... who did change our plans? I smiled as I fell asleep. This was my kind of trip!

Next morning saw us all lining up outside the museum. It was only fifty metres from the hotel! Knowing we were on limited time, I assured them all they would be back later in the trip to spend as much time as they liked, but for now... Akhenaten beckoned!

We headed down to his section and arrived out of breath. Something was happening. I could hardly breathe. The others were having the same problem.

Must have been the plane, I thought. I tuned into Ahkenaton to see why we were summoned and he told me to take a deep breath. I did but was promptly told that was not a deep breath. A much bigger breath gave me a surprising "pop" in my heart as a seal was broken, and my breathing relaxed. He told me to do it to the others. I got to do a few there and the others got their seal broken a bit later. WOW!

We were gathering a short while later to catch the plane to Luxor. I raced back to my room knowing Barbara would have arrived and I found her standing in my clothes. It was really funny as she is at least a foot taller than me! She had been separated from her luggage.

We arrived in Luxor and settled into our hotel, which was right on the Nile, and beautiful. We set off to get Barbara some clothes, which was not easy as most Egyptian woman are also on the short side. However we did meet Ali, who had just bought a small bus and promised to take us wherever we needed to go. We arranged for him to show us his bus that evening before we committed.

It was good and Ali was a fantastic guide.

That evening he took us to the Luxor temple, and we were amazed at the orbs we could see physically; a wonderful "first" look at Egypt!

*Visible orbs with group at Luxor Temple.*

The next day Ali picked us up bright and early and took us to Queen Hatshepsut's temple. My first trip to Egypt was, among other things, to connect with Akhenaten and Queen Hatshepsut. One of my tasks on the first trip was to find a white hieroglyph with a tree in it. After searching far and wide, I finally climbed over a rope and got a close look at a section of Queen Hatshepsut's temple that was being restored. It had white hieroglyphs! Beside the one with the tree in it was a picture of Queen Hatshepsut showing clearly that she had Lymphoedema, the condition that I also have.

Back at her temple again I wondered what would happen. I could hear some toning happening and knowing that some of my group enjoy this I wandered up and found them in a circle. I joined in and as we toned I could feel Queen Hatshepsut's essence being drawn out of the walls until there was enough of her to enable me to channel her message. We had been gifted with the opened heart seal through which we discovered the divine feminine could flow through us. Queen Hatshepsut asked that she accompany us and help download the divine feminine through us. She was very excited as it had been prophesied to her, centuries ago, that she would do this.

Wow; it doesn't get any better than this!

We went on to the Valley of the Kings and then to an authentic Egyptian meal that Ali had organised for us. It was an absolutely fabulous day!

The next day we went to Karnak Temple and with the aid of Queen Hatshepsut, downloaded the divine feminine energy through a special ceremony. The trip was becoming an amazing life force! A bit of light relief in the morning had seen us flying over the Valley of the Kings in a hot air balloon, a must for any tourist!

Ali had promised us a surprise and told us not to be late at our pickup point. He had arranged a trip in a felucca called the Endeavour (for the Aussies he said). We had to be towed as the engines failed but he had provided a fabulous meal which we ate as the sun set over the Nile. We were being very spoilt.

*Feluccas on the Nile River at sunset.*

The next leg of our trip saw us loaded up into a small bus again and we headed to Dendara and Abydos temples. Because we had arranged to visit

Akhenaten's new city, we had to have an armed escort, as it was off the tourist trail and not safe to travel.

We set off with a jeep full of tourist police in front of us, with their machine guns...

Dendara and Abydos are the best temples to visit I think, because there is the first astrological chart at Dendara, and Abydos has the hieroglyphs of a tank and helicopter, neither of which had been invented in those days. Wonderful places to visit, with lots of 11/11 stuff in Abydos.

We had limited time as we had to make it to Amara where we were staying. It was a bit disconcerting as we walked to a restaurant for tea, complete with police and machine gun behind us. What an adventure we were having! Fortunately no one in the group worried about the possible danger. Just knowing we were going to where so few get to go was exciting and special. A magical trip so far...

The next morning saw us heading to Akhenaten's New City. We were amazed to see that most of it had been destroyed, but his tomb was being restored and it told the story of his life with his family. Akhenaten had the elongated skull that many early tribes have, worldwide. His wife Nefertiti also appeared to also have the elongated skull,

I believe that Akhenaten was half Sirian and his height was about eleven feet. He was part of the experiment to unite the planet under one God, but as history will show again and again, the good guys rarely win. They get removed by those whose power is threatened.

When we got to what was left of his temple, we shuffled through the sand and were amazed to be able to pick up pieces of pottery that could have been used by the great king himself!

*Remains of Akhenaten's temple at Amarna*

We wandered in the heat, and the silence. Hardly anyone spoke. The place had such an aura of reverence, which is the only word that I can use to portray what we were feeling.

Nefertiti's temple was more advanced in the restoration work but it didn't have the feeling of reverence.

We noticed the heart pounding and we formed a circle and the Divine Feminine once again flowed into the earth.

*More remains of Akhenaten's temple in Amarna*

## The Great Pyramids

We headed back to Cairo and once again were taken to the Nile Hilton. It just happened to be the World Cup Soccer game that night and Egypt was playing. They won and we witnessed the excitement and passion of the Egyptians. Even the taxi horns were playing out the National Anthem! The party continued all night!

The next day was a rest day and some hit the markets, some went to Alexandria, and some of us went to the museum. I wanted to check in and see if there was any further instructions for our great pyramid visit.

We had timed the pyramid visit for the 11/11/11, and had obtained an hour's private time in the Queen's Chamber, or so I had been assured. Our guide told us that no one had been in the Queen's Chamber for many years.

"What?" This was the climax of our trip and the work we had been asked to do. I stacked on a huge tantrum, but that didn't help. It did get us an hour of private time in the King's Chamber though. I worried that we would not be able to download the divine feminine down through the earth to the waterways that were part of the Nile.

I believe that three other groups were sent to Egypt to do the same task.

Our time in the Great Pyramid was awesome as usual, and the high vibrations were really lifting us to where we needed to be. I felt my new heart chamber start to vibrate and it was through these divine feminine heart chambers that had been opened at the beginning of our tour, that the divine feminine flowed into its destination.

Phew, I was so relieved that we managed to do what was asked of us, and of course the energy flowed into us as well. Also, of course I connected Tasmania to the Pyramid! I looked around at all the shining eyes and faces and thought...yeah!

*The Great Pyramids and the Sphinx*


If the chambers in our hearts hadn't had their seal broken we could not have achieved what we did. Unbelievable? Absolutely! But this is my life!

The Vortex grew with the big Egyptian download; the divine feminine was gaining momentum!

# The Two Become One

Soon after, my long time friend from Phillip Island was over. She had bought the land behind my block some time ago. We had spent a good afternoon with many of her friends putting up the teepee. It was no easy feat even with six people!

*The yurt and the teepee nestled in the forest.*

Jo and I had a meal in front of the teepee and as we sat back and enjoyed the evening, she said,

"My right leg is tingling."

"Wow," I said, "my left leg is tingling," so we went and stood on the male and female vortexes (approximately a hundred metres apart.) We had figured out that the two vortexes would eventually join together. We could feel the energies being drawn through us and when it stopped we went to the central spot and yes there was now a huge energy vortex.

I was surprised that the Vortex hadn't formed a male and female Vortex. It had, but in a different way; there were concentric rings of anti clockwise, clockwise then anti clockwise, or female, male, female, male etc.

I was then shown that the concentric rings caused a rift in the ether, and this is what creates a star gate. A star gate is an entry and exit point from this dimension.

Wow! The Vortex had grown immensely! The energy rings have a distinct pull, forwards or backwards, depending on which ring you are standing on. Everyone can feel this, even the most diehard of sceptics cannot stop the pull with their eyes closed! The ley line has reached over a hundred metres wide.

# What Next? Mission Impossible!

I was nudged by my guidance that we had a task in central Australia. Great! I love Alice Springs.

We had to create a new vortex somewhere between Uluru and Kata't Juta. The hardest part was that I couldn't do the right thing and ask permission to do this on Aboriginal land. The energy had been quite corrupt at Uluru and I was asked to create a male female vortex between the two monoliths. I asked my friend Junitta from the Egyptian adventures, and another few women joined us.

*Kata't Juta in Northern Territory*

Again I had no idea where or how I was to do this, but as usual there was a big distraction provided when a French model decided to run naked on Uluru. All the park rangers raced towards the rock and we found our spot and did what we needed to do. We drew the rainbow serpent from his home in the waterhole at Uluru.

He was not impressed at all and moved very slowly. The serpent of light came from Kata t'Juta and circled us while we waited on the rainbow serpent. He too circled us and eventually they became the Orobus symbol. Phew, the vortex was formed and is a male female vortex!

# Adjustments

Most of 2010 was spent just adjusting to the regular downloads, clearing the debris and settling before the next download.

For the 10/10 we decided to invite as many as wished to come, and many did. It was time for more Vortex adjustments and this one came in the form of another Earth Keeper by the name of Kerry Stewart; a small form with the biggest voice! Her voice rang out through the valley as the energies flowed into the earth via the Vortex and Kerry.

Jackie Rothsay, a pipe carrier from New Zealand, treated us to a wonderful ceremony and all our energies were blended and received; a fabulous day!

*Kerry Stewart with Earthkeeper Sue*

## *SunDisk at Lake Titicaca*

I had become aware of patterns on the ocean in front of us; they were circular, like the ones I had seen on Lake Titicaca, from the Isle of the Sun, the home of one of the Sun Disks.

I tuned into the patterns and felt an odd, but familiar stirring in my solar plexus. I wondered if it could be a Sun Disk, and sent a deep, solar plexus breath to the area, Immediately I felt a huge blast back through my solar plexus! It was a Sun Disk!

*Sun Disk in Tasmania*

Later that year on the Summer Solstice, a few friends had gathered and a wonderful day was had by all. Emily told me that she felt the urge to sing, so with a bit of encouragement she did. The song didn't have words, but sounds. As soon as Emily's beautiful voice rang out, I had a major breakthrough. I knew absolutely everything in that moment (even though I had no idea what I knew). One thing did come through very clearly. It was a vision of me standing on a mountain looking back at Tasmania. I was holding a Sun

Disk and placing it carefully. I could tell that it was long, long ago as there are no mountains looking at Tasmania. There are, however, mountains under the sea. I realized I had done what I set out to do all those years ago. Overwhelmed, I sat down and sobbed. Wow, what a journey this has been!

Then I heard my inner voice saying, "There is more!"

# Birth of the Vortex Healing Centre

The energies continued to grow and change. My career seemed to nosedive from a successful lymphoedema therapist to an out of work depressive!

I was also asked or told by my guidance to build a healing centre on the land but the challenge was ~ No Buildings. I must not leave any footprints!

Barbara was becoming a frequent visitor and by now it was generally accepted she would move over and help me. After much deliberation we decided on yurts. It was a great idea; no council fees, no footprints, good energy in a round space!

*Wet but happy building our yurt!*

And so it was; a yurt! Finding one was proving to be a very expensive exercise with overseas being the only place google could find to source. Hmmm, I was rather broke at the time, a constant in my life thus far! I was walking the dogs and pondering the whys and wherefores of life, when I met up with my neighbour. I shared my tale of woe and she laughed and said that a young guy in St Marys had just started building them. Well what could I say?

*The Yurt lives! A fantastic space with a clear dome.*

Zeb Walker, an artist and creator, made us a fabulous yurt.

Of course on the day we decided to erect it, the rain came and it was a traditional Gray (home town) rain; two inches minimum!

The Vortex Healing Centre was born.

*Celebrating the yurt build is finally done!*

*The small yurt is finished and awaiting guests*

In fact two yurts were born; a small one for accommodation, and one big one for our Healing Centre.

The rain that began in early January continued right throughout the year. It always seemed to be raining. The equinox always manages to bring wet and windy weather and the March Equinox was no exception; record rainfall over three days saw little creeks become raging rivers, dams became lakes, and paddocks were also lakes. Fifteen inches fell over a three day period. Our nearby town of St Marys was flooded, roads were washed away and the house was always full of wet laundry, or so it seemed.

A big cleansing was happening and the water just kept on coming. Our area received over two metres of rain for the year. Nice green paddocks kept Mika the horse very happy!

I also got to visit Barbara in her home town of Mahwah New Jersey. I arrived just in time for a hurricane and spent the time helping her prepare her home for the high winds and heavy rain. It wasn't as bad as I thought it would be, and a bit of a clean-up in the yard and the drying out of the basement put everything back to rights.

I got to see New York and lots of beautiful places in Barbara's area. I was surprised how beautiful it was here. It was no surprise to learn that Barbara's home was on a very powerful ley line.

# 11/11/2011

Another very big day on the Spiritual Calender! We had many come for the big day, and quite a few camped for a few days. A lot of fun was had and the incoming energies were felt by all.

There was a huge activation for many people, especially those that had not been to the Vortex before, or who missed out on some of the upgrades.

People were being drawn to the Vortex now and each having a big healing or an upgrade or both. We were doing all kinds of healing in the yurt and I also was massaging part time from home.

The stage or the Vortex was ready for the big year ahead; 2012 was going to be a stand out year for personal and planetary growth. This can only mean one things, more cleansing and clearing. Mother Earth was doing her cleansing too, with floods and earthquakes etc.

The Vortex was flowing nicely into the role it was chosen for, and that was to purify and cleanse the energies that were coming from all the places to which I had connected the vortex. With lots of good energy to help stabilise the grids, the diamond grid was nearly complete!

We had also discovered that there were more power points on the property and in fact they formed a ground level Southern Cross.

The great southern hemisphere marker is the Southern Cross and is made up of five stars.

As above, so below! The land was really an exciting place to be. As well as the beautiful sea view and the native bush areas, the "New" power sites were proving to have different purposes. The Vortex was the base of the cross, and the other sites will be revealed in stage two of the Vortex history.

*Happy celebrants on the 11/11 at the vortex.*

# Stage One Complete!

I was nearing the end of my second nine year cycle here and as I looked back through my life here I could see the huge number of blind faith leaps I had taken, the buckets of tears that had been shed, both in my clearing and growth and the Vortex's healing and growth. The life of an Earth Keeper is not easy. I had also chosen this life ahead of having a family, given up relationships that were not growing at the rate I was, and gone without a lot of things that make life good. I would choose it all again!

As Tasmania is quite isolated, I was given a couple of ways to share the energies. The first was to charge up crystals and sell them. This also helped to fund the centre. The second was to create essences on the Vortex. These are made from a combination of crystals and wild flowers. Each one has a great healing success rate. They help to remove blockages to growth, working on all four major bodies, mental, physical, emotional and spiritual. These too help to fund the healing centre.

The protection here is very strong and some people are unable to find it!

The fires of 2006 came very close on three occasions, but each time a wind change saved the property. It was a scary time as I had decided to stay and defend! It was pre-Christmas and I discovered eBay while confined for the duration of the fire (ten days).

A mini hurricane went through and did a big detour around the property. I was very well protected!

For the 21/12/2012 we planned a three day camp. We ended up with thirty campers and a few day guests. The fire as usual was the central hub with shared meals and a constantly boiling billy. We had a wonderful time!

We did a big group meditation, and I saw the City of Light which had been above us since 2008, descend into the Vortex area. As it settled many saw huge shards of crystals and felt the warmth of the radiant light.

We all absorbed the energy and our faces were all glowing as we shared what we had felt and seen during the meditation. This meant that the Vortex Area was now residing in the fifth dimension!

What an amazing feeling it was to know that the Vortex had not only achieved its purpose, it could now help to raise many of its connections to the fifth dimension. It also meant the diamond grid was functioning and flowing with the Tasmanian Vortex Energy!

This is the end of this particular stage of the History of the Tasmanian Vortex. The next stage includes the arrival of Barbara, a labyrinth, New Zealand, Easter Island and... the story of how I became one of the thirteen Grandmothers of Australia.

# Afterword

The Tasmanian Vortex is the home of the Vortex Healing Centre, where there are many types of healing modalities available.

It is a non profit organisation, and is funded by the sale of crystals, healing essences (made by a naturopath) and the healing sessions Barbara and I do. Qi gong is a favorite, along with the silent retreats, meditation groups etc.

Visitors are always encouraged to come and experience the energies of the Vortex, and just bliss out in the beautiful surrounds.

We are active on facebook, Vortex Healing Centre Inc and our website www.VortexHealingCentre.com.

Itunes: Vortex energy podcast
Email: vortexhealingcentre@gmail.com

Phone 0418515419.
Facebook vortexhealingcentre7215


A sensitive being will be able to pick up the energies of the vortex from the front cover. An inspired work of art by Carol Matthews.

The image itself is an activator and will help you to connect energetically to the vortex.

Please feel free to check out vortexhealingcentre.com/cover for a free download of the full activated image.

I would love to hear your stories about your vortex.

www.ingramcontent.com/pod-product-compliance
Lightning Source LLC
Chambersburg PA
CBHW071409040426
42444CB00009B/2161